Adult ADHD

The Complete Guide to Living with, Understanding, Improving, and Managing ADHD or ADD as an Adult!

Table of Contents

Introduction 1

Chapter 1: What is ADHD? 2

Chapter 2: Signs and Symptoms of ADHD in Adults 6

Chapter 3: Treatment for Adult ADHD 15

Chapter 4: Living with ADHD: Helpful Daily Tips.................. 20

Conclusion 27

Introduction

I want to thank you and congratulate you for downloading the book, "Adult ADHD".

This book contains helpful information about ADHD, what it is, and how it can affect adults.

ADHD is most often associated with young children, however many people never outgrow the condition and continue to display symptoms throughout adulthood.

For many, ADHD has never been diagnosed and as a result they have never sought treatment.

Whether you personally have ADHD, or a loved one does, this book will help you to better understand the condition as well as its symptoms and side effects.

You will learn about the different treatment methods available, as well as what medical professionals to consult with.

This book will also explain to you tips and techniques that will allow you to manage your or your partner's ADHD as an adult! This includes a breakdown of the medical treatments available, along with self-help methods that you can employ from home.

If you or a loved one are suffering from adult ADHD, then this is the guide for you.

Thanks again for downloading this book, I hope you enjoy it!

Chapter 1:
What is ADHD?

Mention ADHD and what immediately comes to mind is an image of a child who can't sit still, who talks fast, zooms from one activity to another, and is often the cause of commotion in the classroom, playroom or wherever they may be. They're a teacher's nightmare and a challenge for their harried parents, as well.

What a lot of people don't know is that there is an adult version of that scenario. A number of grownups suffer from ADHD too and like many children with the disease, this condition impacts negatively on their work or schooling, relationships and day-to-day life.

What is different between childhood and adult ADHD is that the adults themselves often are not aware that they have the disorder. Adult ADHD is often unrecognized and harder to diagnose. A person usually finds out about it by accident when they seek medical attention for other problems they may have, such as anxiety or depression.

If you suspect that you, or another person close to you, may have ADHD, then this ebook is the perfect guide for you. Here, we will explain what adult ADHD is, its signs and symptoms and the treatment for it. We will also provide tried-and-tested tips on how to manage the disease so that it does not make life too difficult for you and for those who live or work with you.

The Basic Facts About ADHD

To start off, let's get to know what ADHD is and why some people have it.

ADHD stands for "attention deficit/hyperactivity disorder." Sometimes it is referred to as just ADD ("attention deficit disorder"). In the past, medical professionals used the phrase "ADD with or without hyperactivity." It is much easier to say ADHD and that is now the standard term used.

ADHD is a mental health condition characterized chiefly by three things:

- difficulty focusing or maintaining attention on one thing for long
- hyperactivity or restlessness
- impulsive behavior

ADHD starts in early childhood. Adults with the disease had it when they were children, although it's possible they were never diagnosed.

The truth is that everyone, at some point in his life, exhibits the symptoms of ADHD. Sometimes we cannot focus well, or we feel restless, or we give in to an impulse. These are normal behaviors, especially in times of stress or extreme tiredness. It is when these behaviors happen often, and when they become so severe that they cause significant problems in certain areas of a person's life, that it becomes ADHD. For instance, children with ADHD have learning problems because they cannot focus on schoolwork. Adults with the disease often have unstable relationships and have trouble with the law. They may also have problems at work and with alcohol or drug abuse.

It can be difficult to tell whether a person has ADHD or is behaving normally. Not every child who is hyperactive and who has a learning difficulty does have ADHD. Likewise, not every adult who has relationship, career and substance abuse problems has ADHD. In fact, many mood disorders (such as depression and anxiety) are also characterized by behavior patterns similar to those seen in ADHD. How then do psychologists effectively diagnose the disease?

The criteria for diagnosing ADHD are listed in the Diagnostic and Statistical Manual of Mental Disorders (DSM), a standard reference book used by psychologists and mental health workers. Listed here are symptoms falling under the two main categories of "inattention" and "hyperactivity and impulsivity." If a person has at least six of those symptoms (from one or both categories), they are diagnosed with ADHD. (We will look at the symptoms in adults more closely in later chapters.)

As for what causes the condition, the activity of brain chemicals called neurotransmitters play a major role. Studies reveal that in people with ADHD, these neurotransmitters are less active in areas of the brain that are responsible for attention and focus. To use a medical term, people with ADHD have problems with "executive function"—mental skills performed by the frontal lobe of the brain to control certain behaviors. We actually use executive function for many things, not just to focus. We also use it to plan, organize, manage time, remember details, make judgments and decisions, curb inappropriate impulses, work towards a goal, function as an independent individual, and so on.

If our executive function is impaired, our brain would have problems carrying out its "organization" and "regulation" tasks. Our brain "organizes" by gathering information to be evaluated. It then "regulates" by judging and adapting our behavior to that judgment. To illustrate, seeing a chocolate cake and feeling tempted to eat it is an organizing activity of the brain. Deciding that it is not a good idea to have that cake and walking away is a regulating task.

No one knows what causes the chemical imbalance or the impairment of executive function in the brain that gives rise to ADHD. There are theories that it is genetic. ADHD can indeed run in families. Another possible cause is brain damage due to head injuries, strokes, or diseases such as Alzheimer's. There are studies that also link prenatal exposure to alcohol and cigarettes to impaired brain development and childhood ADHD.

What is certain is that ADHD cannot be prevented and it cannot be cured either. However, it is possible to manage it. There are many coping strategies that the person can learn and use to deal with the difficulties and challenges of having the disease. Psychotherapy, medications and certain modifications in their surroundings and activities can all help immensely to ensure that the sufferer lives as normally as possible.

An adult with ADHD has obvious advantages that a child with the same disease does not have. An adult can take an active role in the treatment of their disorder. Even the simple diagnosis of ADHD can help to explain many things for them, such as why they keep repeating unhealthy patterns of behavior that harm their career and relationships and diminish their chances for happiness and success.

Knowing that you have a mental disorder that you also have the power to manage can provide great relief. It can be the starting point to a whole new life for—one that is happier, calmer, more focused, and much less stressful than what has ever been experienced before.

Chapter 2:
Signs and Symptoms of ADHD in Adults

If you know a person well, you can generally tell if they have ADHD based on some telltale characteristics or symptoms. Here is a quick checklist to help identify an adult with ADHD:

- They are often late for work appointments and social engagements.

- They are impulsive.

- They are disorganized.

- They find it hard to complete tasks on time.

- They are a chronic procrastinator.

- They drive recklessly or ignore traffic rules.

- They cannot focus or concentrate on one thing for long.

- They are restless.

- They become frustrated easily.

- They have frequent mood swings, and often become angry or irritated very quickly.

- They have a low tolerance for stress.

- They have unstable relationships.

- They have a low self-esteem.

A lot of people are guilty of one, two or even a few of the things in the list above. It doesn't immediately mean that they have ADHD. However, it can be a cause for concern if a person has three-fourths or more of those characteristics in the list. If they do, and were diagnosed with ADHD as a child, there is a good chance that they also have ADHD as an adult. The same conclusion holds true even if they were not actually diagnosed with childhood ADHD, but their parents or teachers suspected that they might have it.

According to mental health professionals, all adults with ADHD had it when they were children, even if it was never diagnosed. Statistics also indicate that up to 40% of children with ADHD continue to have the mental disorder when they grow into adulthood. Some of these adults may now exhibit fewer or milder symptoms than they did when they were young. Others may continue to show unmistakable symptoms, which in turn can cause significant problems in certain areas of their life, especially in their career and relationships.

Let's look more closely at the top symptoms of ADHD in adults in the sections below.

Risk factors for ADHD

A person has an increased risk of adult ADHD if any of the following is true:

- They have a parent, sibling or any blood relative who has ADHD or another mental disorder (such as depression, anxiety or bipolar disorder).

- Their mother, while pregnant with them, smoked, used drugs or drank alcohol.

- During their mother's pregnancy with them, she was exposed to environmental poisons such as polychlorinated biphenyls or PCBs.

- When they were a child, they were exposed to environmental toxins, such as lead (in the paint on toys) and in old pipes.

- They had a premature birth.

General symptoms of ADHD in adults

The most common symptoms seen in adults with ADHD are:

- Difficulty concentrating and sustaining focus
- Trouble with prioritizing activities or planning
- Disorganization and messiness
- Forgetfulness and constantly losing things
- Impatience or restlessness
- Impulsivity
- Chronic lateness for work and important events
- Being easily distracted
- Lack of self-control (which includes the inability to control impulses, anger, and rude or inappropriate behavior)
- Being easily bored when doing dull or routine activities

- Selective hyperfocus, or the ability to focus intently on something that they find enjoyable or interesting

- Low tolerance for stress and frustration

- Low self-esteem, insecurity and feelings of inferiority or underachievement

These symptoms produce unwanted consequences. Very often, the negative outcomes of those symptoms include:

- Missed deadlines and non-completion of tasks started

- Forgetting to attend meetings or show up for social engagements

- Poor job performance (or poor academic performance if the person is in school)

- Inability to hold down a job for long

- Stress-induced anxiety or depression

- Mood swings and quick bursts of anger – These are often the result of feeling restless, bored or impatient, such as when waiting in line and driving in heavy traffic.

- Unstable relationships – Problems arise when those around the person with ADHD constantly nag them to be more tidy or organized, and when they become hurt and resentful of the person's behavior to the point that they perceive to be insensitive and irresponsible.

- Awkwardness in social settings

- Trouble with the law

- Substance abuse (alcohol or drugs)

- Financial problems (due mainly to the lack of a steady job and impulsive spending)

- Physical health issues (may be due to compulsive eating, substance abuse, skipping doctor's appointments and forgetting to take important medications)

- Mental health problems (brought about by chronic stress, anxiety and low self-esteem)

- Frequent accidents (especially vehicular mishaps)

Experiencing these symptoms and their consequences is, of course, not enough to confirm the presence of ADHD. Only the expert diagnosis by a licensed mental health professional can do that. Careful diagnosis is essential, given that ADHD can easily be mistaken for other psychological conditions or mental disorders. Furthermore, ADHD also often occurs along with these other psychological issues, at the same time and in the same person. These other psychological conditions include:

- Learning disabilities that are seen in people who perform poorly in school and who score very low for their age on academic and intelligence tests

- Personality disorders including antisocial and borderline personality disorders

- Mood disorders such as depression and bipolar (manic-depressive) disorder

- Anxiety disorders such as panic, obsessive-compulsive and social anxiety disorders

Given that ADHD may be mistaken for any of these disorders, and that it can in fact occur simultaneously alongside them, it is imperative that any person suspected of having ADHD should get professional diagnosis and treatment as soon as possible. A good first step for them would be to consult the family doctor. The doctor may then refer them to a good mental health specialist (a psychologist or a psychiatrist) for further testing.

Criteria for the Diagnosis of ADHD in Adults

As mentioned earlier, psychologists rely (among other things) on a standard list of criteria for ADHD that is provided in the Diagnostic and Statistical Manual of Mental Disorders (DSM) of the American Psychiatric Association (APA). The full list of those criteria is given below, grouped into two categories. As pointed out earlier, a person must exhibit at least six of these characteristics or symptoms for them to be diagnosed with ADHD.

Symptoms that Show Inattention:

1. The person often fails to pay enough attention to detail, which results in careless mistakes at work or when doing other activities.

2. They have trouble focusing for long on a single task.

3. They frequently do not appear to listen when directly spoken to.

4. They habitually fail to finish tasks or assignments, or fails to follow through on instructions.

5. They often find it hard to organize tasks and activities.

6. They dislike, and so often avoid, activities that require sustained mental attention.

7. They frequently lose things, especially items that are essential to complete tasks or activities.

8. Distractions easily sidetrack them.

9. They often forget things and details, or fails to do chores or show up for appointments because they have forgotten

Symptoms that Show Hyperactivity or Impulsivity:

1. They often cannot sit still; they fidget or squirm in their seat.

2. During meetings, lectures and other activities where people are seated, they often get up to leave the room whenever they can.

3. They cannot or do not restrain their restlessness and physical activity even when such behavior is inappropriate.

4. They often talk or move around while doing leisure activities.

5. Their restlessness makes it seem like they are "driven" and have an endless supply of energy.

6. Most people around them frequently accuse them of "talking too much."

7. They are fond of interrupting other people or intruding on their private conversations.

8. They often blurt out a response before someone finishes asking a question.

9. They find it hard to wait for their turn. They become impatient in queues or when told to wait.

Psychologists don't solely depend on the checklist above, even though it is very useful, to arrive at a diagnosis of adult ADHD. They also consider these additional symptoms and criteria:

- The person must have exhibited the symptoms of ADHD for at least six successive months.

- The symptoms are severe enough to cause problems in the workplace, in school or at home. The symptoms also put a strain on the person's relationships with family members and other people.

- More or less the same symptoms were also present when the person was a child or adolescent.

To find out if a person has the symptoms of the disorder, the psychologist carefully interviews them and asks them to answer questionnaires and tests. They also inquire about the person's diet and any medications or drugs they take, as these could give rise to ADHD-like symptoms. They may also talk with the patient's family members and close friends. Based on all that, the psychologist examines the effects of the symptoms, if any, to the person's current life. They try to find out in particular if the symptoms have an effect on the person's work performance and relationships.

The result of the diagnosis indicates if the patient does have ADHD or not. Alongside a positive diagnosis, the psychologist also comes up with useful insights regarding how the disorder affects the patient's life on a day-to-day basis. The findings, furthermore, explain if the person also suffers from other psychological issues, such as learning disabilities or other mental disorders.

Chapter 3:
Treatment for Adult ADHD

As with all mental disorders (and physical conditions as well), it is best if treatment is given at the earliest possible time. This will prevent further progression of the disease, and provide much needed relief to the person who is likely heavily weighed down by the strain of dealing with their condition. The people around them will also experience some relief, as ADHD affects the people who work and live with the person who has the disorder.

If the person with ADHD does not receive proper treatment for one reason or another, then they will likely continue to have problems in many areas of life. Their physical and mental health, work, finances and relationships will be in jeopardy for as long as they have untreated ADHD. In fact, their problems in these areas will potentially build up and escalate with the passing of time if they do not do anything about the disorder.

An immediate benefit of treatment for many ADHD patients is immense relief. As previously mentioned, this can be felt as early as when a positive diagnosis of the condition is made. The person will feel relieved to know that they are not to blame for being irresponsible, impulsive, rude, insensitive, unemployed or underemployed, and for many other shortcomings they may or may not have. They now know that their difficulties and failures are the symptoms of a mental disorder with real treatment options available. They did not happen because of a character flaw or a personal weakness.

With that said, much remains to be done to keep the ADHD under control. As pointed out earlier, the disease cannot be cured, but it can be managed such that the symptoms are kept to a minimum. However, it can often take many months, even years, for the treatment to be 100% successful.

There are two basic treatment approaches. The first is with the use of medications and the second is through counseling or "talk therapy." These approaches may be combined, or only one of them may be applied. It depends on the severity of the symptoms experienced and the progress of the treatment process, which a mental health professional will closely monitor. Generally, a psychologist will recommend counseling only, while a psychiatrist will likely suggest both medications and talk therapy simultaneously.

Medications for ADHD

Stimulants are the most common medicines used to treat ADHD. This comes as a surprise for many people since it seems counterproductive to offer stimulants to a person who is already hyperactive or "over-stimulated." However, stimulants are effective in that they enhance focus and concentration. At the same time, they also decrease distractibility. These medicines work by modifying brain activity, specifically by altering the circuits in the brain that control attention. They also help to balance neurotransmitters in the brain.

Some examples of stimulants for ADHD are:

- methylphenidate (Ritalin, Concerta, Metadate)
- dextroamphetamine-amphetamine (Adderall XR)
- lisdexamfetamine (Vyvanse)
- dextroamphetamine (Dexedrine)

These are often taken orally daily. At times, the doctor may prescribe a long-acting form of the stimulant drug, such as a skin patch, instead of daily tablet or pill doses. This is because many ADHD patients have trouble remembering to take their medicines at a certain time every day. Their noncompliance to the scheduled daily intake of medications can hamper the treatment process.

Stimulants primarily ease the symptoms of inattention and hyperactivity. To reduce and control impulsive behavior, another kind of medication is used, namely selective norepinephrine reuptake inhibitors. An example of this is Atomoxetine (Strattera).

Health professionals may also prescribe antidepressants and mood stabilizers, especially if stimulants do not work as well as expected. A common antidepressant is bupropion (Wellbutrin).

Stimulants often work fast and produce dramatic improvement within a day or two. In fact, many people attest that they feel they can concentrate better within a half-hour of taking a stimulant medicine.

In comparison to stimulants, other types of ADHD medications typically work more slowly, taking weeks before they become fully effective. However, they are more preferable for people who have a history of substance abuse and who cannot tolerate the side effects of stimulants.

It is necessary to follow what the doctor prescribes in terms of dosage and timing (when to take the medicine). They may later adjust the dosage or even change the medication, depending on how effective the drug turns out to be and the side effects observed. It may take some time before the doctor finds out what is exactly right for a patient.

Psychological Counseling for ADHD

Taking medications is generally effective in reducing or easing the major symptoms associated with ADHD. However, they are not enough to treat the disorder entirely. They don't do anything, for instance, to correct the person's low self-esteem or unhealthy habits. Counseling or talk therapy is what helps to modify these and other more deeply rooted psychological issues.

In the treatment of ADHD, the prime focus of counseling is to help the patient improve their organization skills, manage their time well, learn better social skills, mend relationships, and develop helpful daily routines. Counseling will also help them learn how to control their temper and impulsive behavior, improve self-esteem, cope with past failures and develop effective problem-solving skills. Counseling is hugely beneficial in so many ways, especially in the specific area or problem where the patient has the greatest difficulty. Typically, the therapist identifies the major problem areas for a patient first and concentrates on addressing those.

There are many types of psychological counseling. The ones that seem to be most helpful for ADHD patients are these two:

- Cognitive behavioral therapy (CBT) - This is a popular method that enables the person to acquire coping skills useful for day-to-day living. It helps them to manage their behavior and modify unhealthy or harmful thinking patterns into more positive ones. It also helps the person to deal better with any mental health issues they may have such as depression, anxiety or drug abuse. CBT sessions are often done one-on-one, that is, with just the therapist and the patient interacting. Other CBT sessions are done in a group, with many patients participating.

- Marital counseling and family therapy – This helps the person who has ADHD, as well as their spouse or partner and loved ones. The patient's family members are taught coping strategies to help them handle the stress of living with a person who has ADHD. They also learn how they can help them cope and get better. This kind of counseling improves communication, problem-solving and coping skills.

Chapter 4:
Living with ADHD: Helpful Daily Tips

While a person is being treated for ADHD, they can do many things on their own to reduce the symptoms they have and live as normal a life as possible. In this chapter are some tips and advice that they can put into immediate use to help keep the symptoms of the disorder under control.

General Tips and Guidelines for Living with ADHD

- Have a positive attitude towards the disease. This simply means that a person should not regard having ADHD as a hopeless situation that makes it impossible for them to be successful or happy in their work, relationships and family life. It is more positive and constructive to think of ADHD as a unique assortment of personality traits or characteristics. Some of these traits are helpful, while others are not so. Those with ADHD can be very creative, passionate, energetic and enthusiastic. They can think out of the box and come up with original ideas that others cannot.

- As you acknowledge your strengths, you should also get to know your major weaknesses. Is being impulsive your biggest problem? Is procrastination and chronic tardiness causing your work to suffer? Just knowing what you need to work on focuses your efforts and this makes it easier to deal with the problems.

- Look after your physical health. Like everyone else, you need to exercise regularly and eat well. Vigorous exercise is in fact very helpful in working off some of the excess energy and aggression that most people with ADHD have. Eat a healthy diet and avoid food items that can aggravate your mood swings. In particular, stay away from highly sweetened foods, coffee and alcoholic beverages. Also, remember to get lots of sleep. When you are tired and sleep-deprived, it will be much harder to concentrate, do your work and stay on top of your responsibilities. You should sleep for seven or eight hours every night.

- If you can, join support groups for people with ADHD. Here, you can meet other people like yourself and share experiences and useful information such as coping strategies. There are support groups in many communities, as well as online.

- Ask for help from family, friends or co-workers if you need it. When you feel overwhelmed, reach out to your therapist or to a loved one for support.

Time Management and Organization Tips

Here is some practical advice that a person with ADHD can use to improve their organization skills and stay on top of responsibilities.

- Set deadlines for all tasks, including chores and minor tasks. Important tasks as well as more routine or minor ones equally tend to be ignored or forgotten by a person with ADHD. Keep track of them all in a planner or some other useful organization tool. Use timers, alarms and reminders as much as possible. The electronic versions of these in smartphones and mobile devices can be very useful. Other people find that handwritten notes work best for them. Use what works for you.

- Have a notebook or electronic device handy at all times so that you can jot down ideas, reminders, or anything that you want to remember later. Review what you have written periodically throughout, and at the end of the day.

- Use lists as often as possible. These include to-do lists, reminders, and notes-to-self lists.

- Have a calendar or appointment book, and place it at eye level, on your desk or wherever you can easily see it. Highlight important deadlines and appointments.

- Prioritize time-sensitive tasks. Set schedules and deadlines for them to "force" yourself to attend to them.

- Whenever possible, deal with a chore right away. If paperwork or a list of to-do's piles up, you may feel overwhelmed and be tempted to procrastinate or just ignore them.

- Experiment to find out which produces better results for you: multi-tasking or single-tasking (doing one task at a time).

- Remember to take breaks at regular times to relieve the monotony of some tasks.

- At the start of every day, make a list of your to-dos. Put at the top of the list the most important tasks and do them at the earliest possible time (early in the morning). During the day, refer many times to this list to make sure that you don't forget any task. It is also very important to be realistic when making your to-do list. List down only what you can accomplish within the day. Don't try to do too much.

- If a task seems too large and daunting, break it down into smaller, more manageable steps.

- Use post-its. The more colorful and visible they are, the better. Stick them everywhere you can see them: at your work desk, on the refrigerator, on bathroom mirrors and in the car.

- Set up a filing system that works for you.

- Have a place for everything and put everything in its proper place. This will help prevent you from losing things and forgetting where they are.

- Have a routine for work or for doing what you need to do, and keep with it consistently.

- If you can, choose to engage in a line of work that interests or motivates you. Many people with ADHD are highly successful in sales, show business or acting, photography, athletic coaching and the military.

- Consider hiring a job coach or asking a mentor to help you if you have difficulties on the job.

Tips Regarding Diet

There isn't a special diet for ADHD, but health experts agree that the considerations below can help keep the symptoms of the disease under better control:

- Protein is important for optimum brain function. It helps in improving focus, concentration and memory. Include high-protein foods in your diet, such as meat, beans, eggs and nuts.

- Essential fatty acids are also important brain foods. Include fish such as tuna and salmon in your diet, as these are good sources of omega-3 fatty acids.

- To reduce mood swings and stabilize energy, stay away from simple carbs and high-sugar foods. Instead, eat complex carbs such as whole-grain pasta and brown rice.

- Eliminate or reduce food items that may stimulate hyperactivity. These are coffee, sugar, junk food and foods that have high preservative content (including food colorings and artificial additives).

- Eat a variety of healthy foods to ensure that you do not miss out on any nutrient.

- There are no specific vitamins, minerals or herbal supplements that have been found out to significantly reduce the symptoms of ADHD. You can take a daily multivitamin supplement to maintain general health, but don't overdose on any particular nutrient. It is also best to consult your doctor before taking herbal supplements just to be on the safe side.

Tips on Improving Relationships

- Schedule time to be with your friends or loved ones.

- Keep engagements. Put them in your calendar and use reminders so that you won't forget them.

- When talking to someone, focus on the conversation and look at the person. Practice good listening skills. Do not interrupt others and do not speak so fast that others cannot understand you.

- If needed, attend couples therapy or marriage/family counseling.

- Let other people know that you have ADHD so that they can better understand your situation and the struggles that you have.

- Listen to what the people close to you are saying, even when they seem to be nagging or trying to control your life. Understand that if you are having difficulties in the relationship, they are too. It is not easy to live with someone who has ADHD. Both parties have to be patient, understanding and sympathetic.

- Continue with your treatment plan, making sure that you take your medications as prescribed and attend all counselling sessions. When the treatment becomes effective, you will notice a significant reduction in the symptoms that put a strain on your relationships. This will in turn make it easier for you and your loved ones to live together more harmoniously.

Alternative interventions for ADHD

There isn't much scientific evidence showing that alternative methods help to relieve the symptoms of ADHD, but some people report that they derive some benefits from such methods. It won't therefore hurt to try these alternative therapies. However, they should never replace the treatment that your psychologist or psychotherapist provides.

Below are some non-conventional interventions that you can explore:

- Yoga and relaxation techniques – These are great for stress relief, and may help a person with ADHD to relax better and reduce restless behavior.

- Meditation – Like yoga, this helps to relieve restlessness and stress. Different types of meditation exist, such as breathing meditation and insight or mindfulness meditation. You can attend a class or follow instructions from an online or live instructor.

- Neuro-feedback training – This involves the use of an EEG machine to monitor your brain wave patterns while you are engaged in a certain task. The purpose is to stimulate and keep active the brain waves in the frontal area of the brain. It can be recalled that people with ADHD have reduced executive function that is controlled by the frontal lobe of the brain. More research needs to be done to determine if neuro-feedback training is indeed helpful for people with ADHD.

Conclusion

Thank you again for downloading this book!

I hope this book was able to help you learn more about Adult ADHD!

The next step is to put this information to use, and begin using the strategies provided to improve and manage your ADHD.

Remember to consult a medical professional before diagnosing or attempting to treat ADHD. Follow their advice, along with the suggestions in this book, and you'll be well on your way to improving your ADHD!

Finally, if you enjoyed this book, please take the time to share your thoughts and post a review on Amazon. It'd be greatly appreciated!

Thank you and good luck!

www.ingramcontent.com/pod-product-compliance
Lightning Source LLC
LaVergne TN
LVHW021748060526
838200LV00052B/3532